DOCTORS IN ACTION

The ANESTHESIOLOGIST

by
Sally G. Ward

**Photographs by
Jackie Baer**

BLACKBIRCH PRESS, INC.
WOODBRIDGE, CONNECTICUT

Published by Blackbirch Press, Inc.
260 Amity Road
Woodbridge, CT 06525

©1999 by Blackbirch Press, Inc.
First Edition

e-mail: staff@blackbirch.com
Web site: www.blackbirch.com

Printed in the United States

10 9 8 7 6 5 4 3 2 1

Library of Congress Cataloging-in-Publication Data
Ward, Sally G.
Anesthesiologist/ by Sally Ward. — 1st ed.
        p.   cm. — (Doctors in action.)
     Summary: Uses the daily activities of one doctor to describe the work of an anesthesiologist.
     Includes bibliographical references and index.
     ISBN 1-56711-233-1 (library binding : alk. paper)
     1. Anesthesiology—Juvenile literature. [1. Anesthesiologists. 2. Occupations.]
I. Title. II. Series.
RD82.W375 1999   98-9875
617.9′6—dc21   CIP
                                                              AC

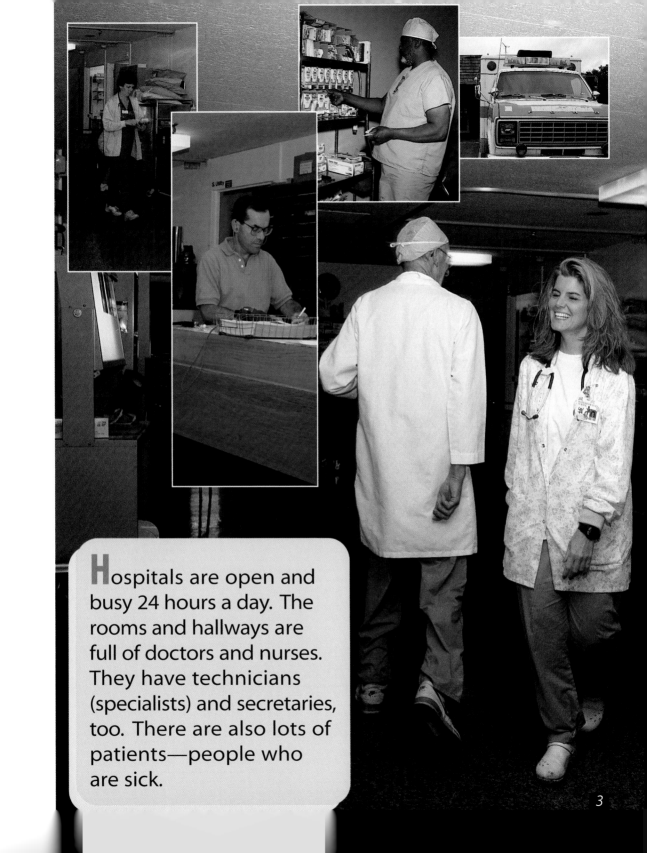

Hospitals are open and busy 24 hours a day. The rooms and hallways are full of doctors and nurses. They have technicians (specialists) and secretaries, too. There are also lots of patients—people who are sick.

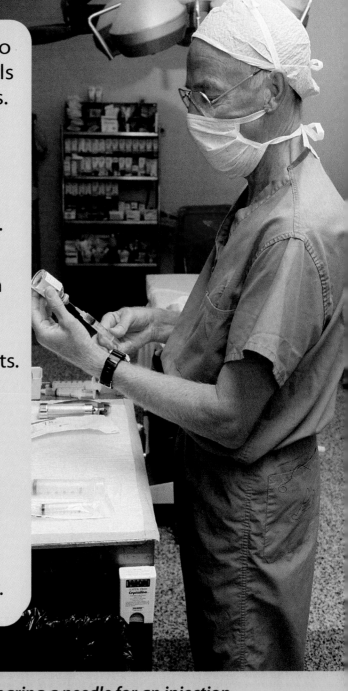

Not many people want to go to the hospital. Hospitals make most people nervous. "Is it going to hurt? Will I feel anything?" That's the first thing people want to know when they are told they will need an operation.

An operation involves several people. Each person has a special job to do. Besides the surgeon, there are operating room assistants. There are nurses and X-ray technicians. There is also an anesthesiologist (an·ess·THEEZ·ee·ol·o·gist). The anesthesiologist's job is to make sure the patient feels no pain. Anesthesia is a special group of drugs that block pain in the body.

Preparing a needle for an injection.
Opposite: *Setting up some machines.*

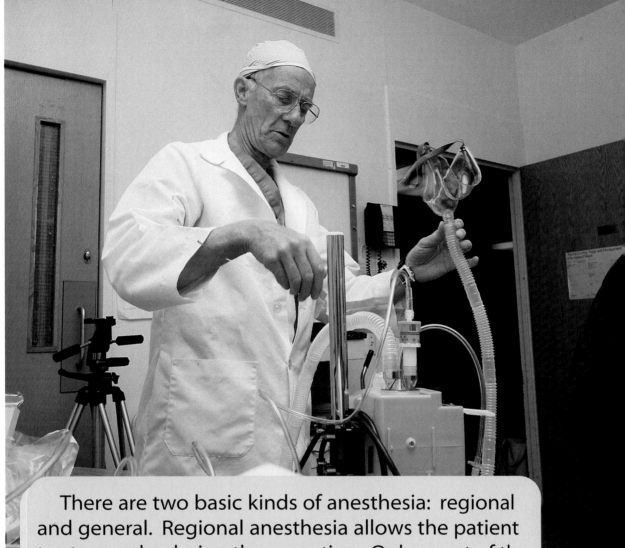

There are two basic kinds of anesthesia: regional and general. Regional anesthesia allows the patient to stay awake during the operation. Only a part of the body goes numb (has no feeling). Regional anesthesia is most often given to a patient as a "shot."

General anesthesia puts the patient to sleep. He or she is "unconscious" and feels nothing at all. The anesthesiologist usually does general anesthesia with a mix of drugs. Some are given by needle. Others are given as a gas. Usually, this is an odorless gas that the patient breathes in.

Dr. Malcolm Dunkley has been an anesthesiologist for more than 30 years. Every day is a new adventure for him.

"For me, every case is different. There are surgeons who only operate on bones. Surgeons who only do ears, noses, or throats. There are heart surgeons and brain surgeons. But an anesthesiologist must be ready and able to work on every type of procedure."

Being an anesthesiologist is a tough job. An anesthesiologist often has to go without food for up to 12 or 13 hours. He or she is not even free to go to the bathroom too much. Other operating room (O.R.) workers can come and go, but the anesthesiologist never leaves the patient.

Dr. Dunkley starts his day with a run before dawn. After a shower and a light breakfast, he's off to the hospital. There, he checks in at the operating room desk to see the list for the day's surgery.

There have been two new cases added since yesterday. The operating room supervisor tells him that Dr. Jacobs is on his way to the O.R.

In the doctor's changing room, Dr. Dunkley quickly changes out of his regular clothes. He puts on fresh, germ-free (sterile) O.R. pants and a shirt. Next he puts on the special sneakers he keeps there. He covers them with sterile O.R. "booties." Since there are no pockets in his O.R. clothes, Dr. Dunkley tucks a five dollar bill in his sock. That's for lunch, later.

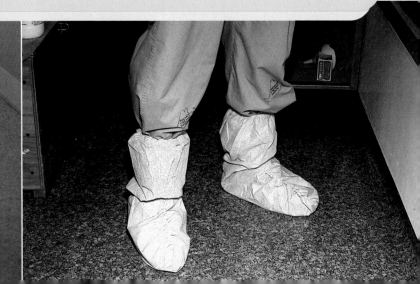

His first scheduled case is with Dr. Jacobs and his patient Mrs. Kingsley. At 8:00 A.M. Mrs. Kingsley is having an operation on her intestine. First Dr. Dunkley reviews her chart (medical record). Then he talks with Mrs. Kingsley. She is concerned about the pain of surgery. Dr. Dunkley explains that it is his job to make sure she doesn't feel anything.

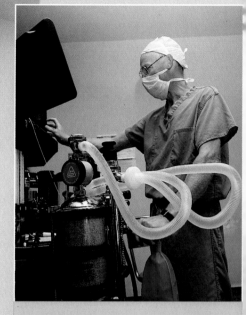

Setting up for an operation.

Dr. Dunkley asks Mrs. Kingsley lots of questions. How tall is she? What is her weight? This information helps him figure out how much anesthesia she will need. The bigger the person, the more they will need.

After talking with Dr. Jacobs, Dr. Dunkley goes to the scrubbing room. There, he washes his hands thoroughly. He uses a special soap that kills germs. Then he goes into the O.R. The nurses have already wheeled Mrs. Kingsley in.

"We'll have you out of here in no time," he tells her. "Don't worry."

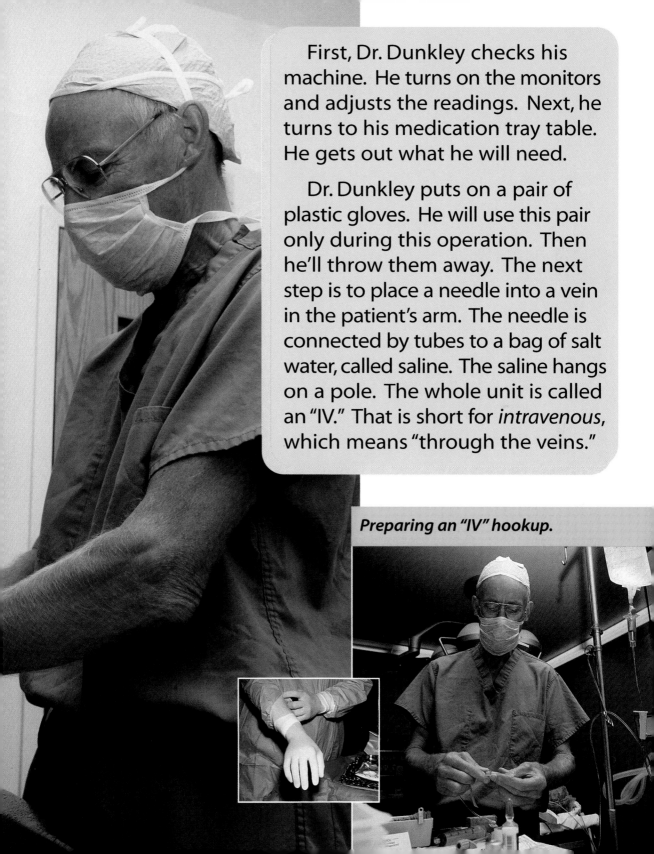

First, Dr. Dunkley checks his machine. He turns on the monitors and adjusts the readings. Next, he turns to his medication tray table. He gets out what he will need.

Dr. Dunkley puts on a pair of plastic gloves. He will use this pair only during this operation. Then he'll throw them away. The next step is to place a needle into a vein in the patient's arm. The needle is connected by tubes to a bag of salt water, called saline. The saline hangs on a pole. The whole unit is called an "IV." That is short for *intravenous*, which means "through the veins."

Preparing an "IV" hookup.

"I hardly felt a thing," says Mrs. Kingsley, after the IV is set up.

Next, Dr. Dunkley wraps a blood pressure cuff around Mrs. Kingsley's arm. After that, he puts flat heart monitoring "sticky buttons" on her chest. He clips a pulse monitor onto her finger. All these are attached to Dr. Dunkley's work station. They will give him constant information. They will tell him how Mrs. Kingsley is reacting to the surgery and to the anesthesia they have chosen.

Dr. Dunkley tells Mrs. Kingsley they are ready to begin. He injects the first dose of anesthesia into the plastic IV tubing. As the liquid enters Mrs. Kingsley's veins, she begins to fall asleep.

Dr. Dunkley places a mask over Mrs. Kingsley's nose and mouth. This is attached by tubes to an anesthesia machine. About an hour goes by. "Have they started yet?" Mrs. Kingsley asks, sleepily, as she wakes up.

"They're already done," says Dr. Dunkley. "It's nearly 9:30 A.M. You'll be home for supper."

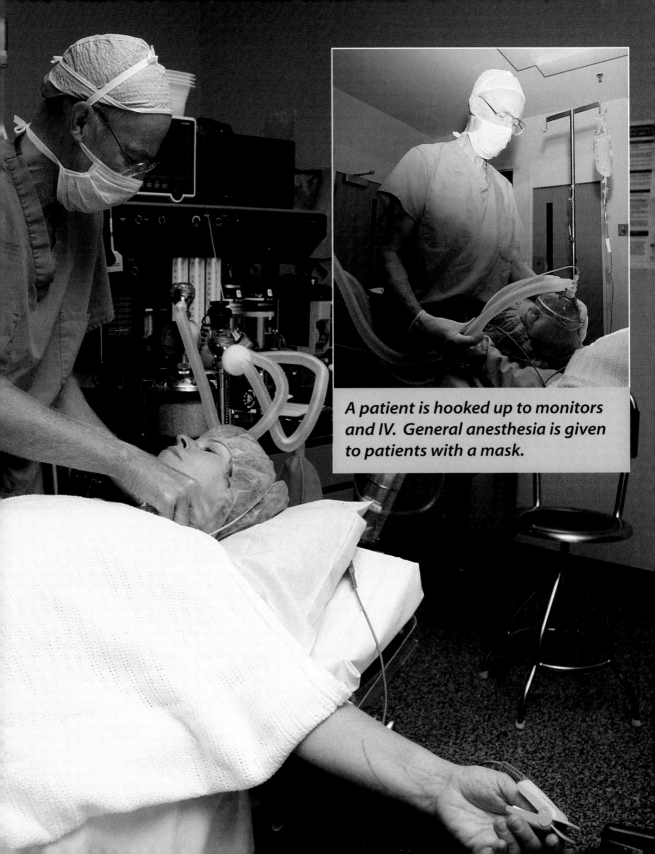

A patient is hooked up to monitors and IV. General anesthesia is given to patients with a mask.

By noon, Dr. Dunkley has finished two more operations. One operation removed a gall bladder. Another, removed the tonsils and adenoids of a two-year-old boy. All the patients are resting comfortably in the recovery room.

There is just time to check in on yesterday's patients before grabbing a bite of lunch in the cafeteria.

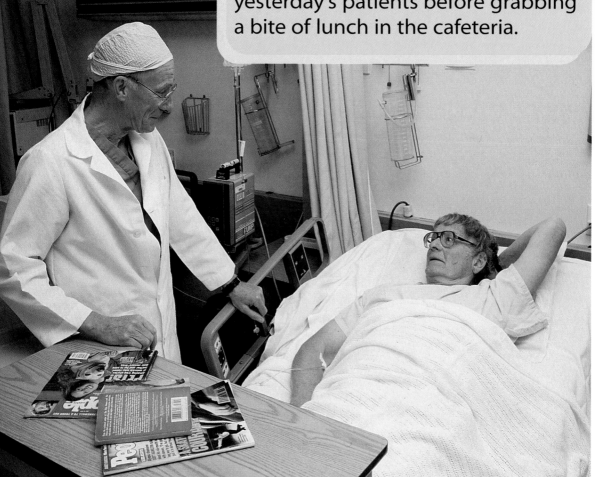

A patient speaks with Dr. Dunkley after surgery.

Suddenly Dr. Dunkley's beeper goes off. He's needed in the emergency room (E.R.). There's a young girl coming in by ambulance. She's having trouble breathing.

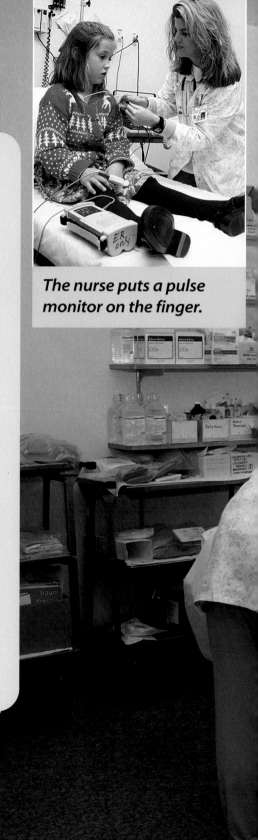

The nurse puts a pulse monitor on the finger.

Dr. Dunkley arrives just as the ambulance pulls up. The nurses move quickly to get the little girl into an examining room.

While the nurse puts on a pulse monitor, Dr. Dunkley asks if this has happened before. "Yes," the mother tells him. "This is Lydia's third asthma attack."

Dr. Dunkley works quickly. He attaches an oxygen mask and heart monitoring buttons. He talks quietly to reassure the family. Soon the readings on the heart monitor show Lydia is improving. The oxygen mask with added medication is helping to restore Lydia's breathing to normal. The whole family feels much better now. After discussing treatment for her asthma with other doctors, Lydia will be able to go home.

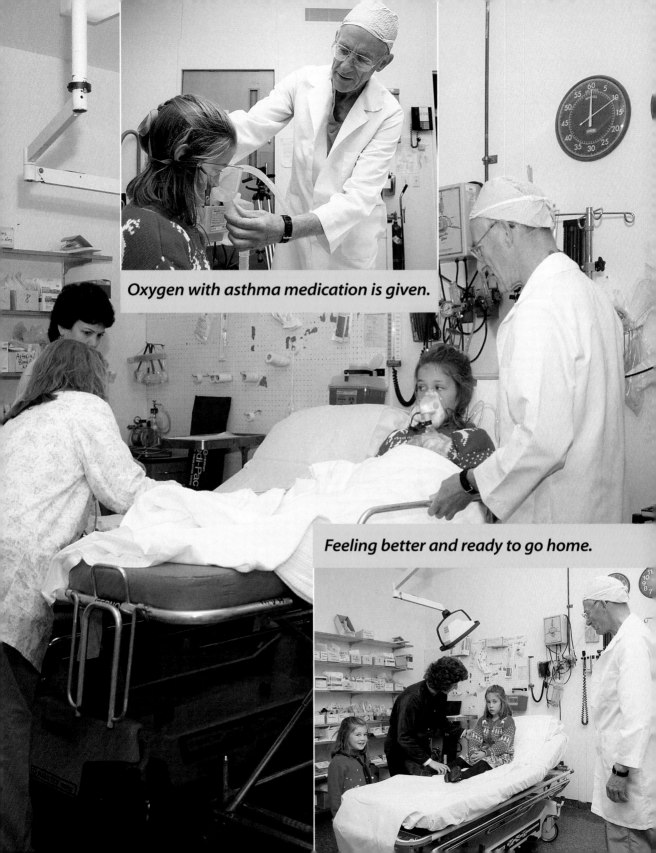

Oxygen with asthma medication is given.

Feeling better and ready to go home.

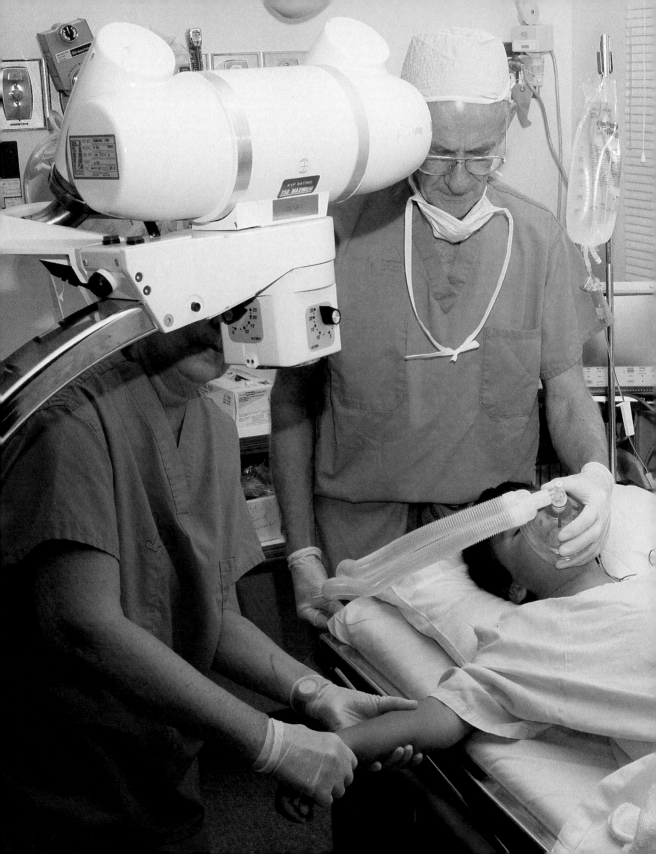

Now Dr. Dunkley is needed back in surgery. A six-year-old boy, Evan, has been waiting since 10:00 A.M. to have his broken arm repaired. The reason he had to wait is an important one. When his mother brought Evan to the hospital, the boy had eaten breakfast only an hour earlier. Before Dr. Dunkley can give patients general anesthesia, their stomachs have to be empty. This usually takes at least four hours. It is very important that this anesthesia safety precaution is taken. It ensures that no food can come up into the throat or mouth and cause choking.

The operating room is set up. This is the one with the large X-ray machine especially for fractures. After he puts on his disposable gloves, Dr. Dunkley prepares Evan. First he sets up an IV tube. Then he attaches heart monitors, a blood pressure cuff, and a pulse monitor.

"I'm going to put you to sleep, now, Evan," says Dr. Dunkley, "but just for a few minutes." He begins to add anesthesia to the IV tube.

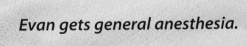

Evan gets general anesthesia.

When the surgeon places Evan's broken arm in position on the X-ray machine, it shows a clean break. After re-setting the bone, they will only need to wrap the arm in a cast and place it in a sling to keep it in line. When Evan wakes up, it is all over. His mother is there waiting. Dr. Dunkley makes sure Evan is feeling all right, then he says good-bye.

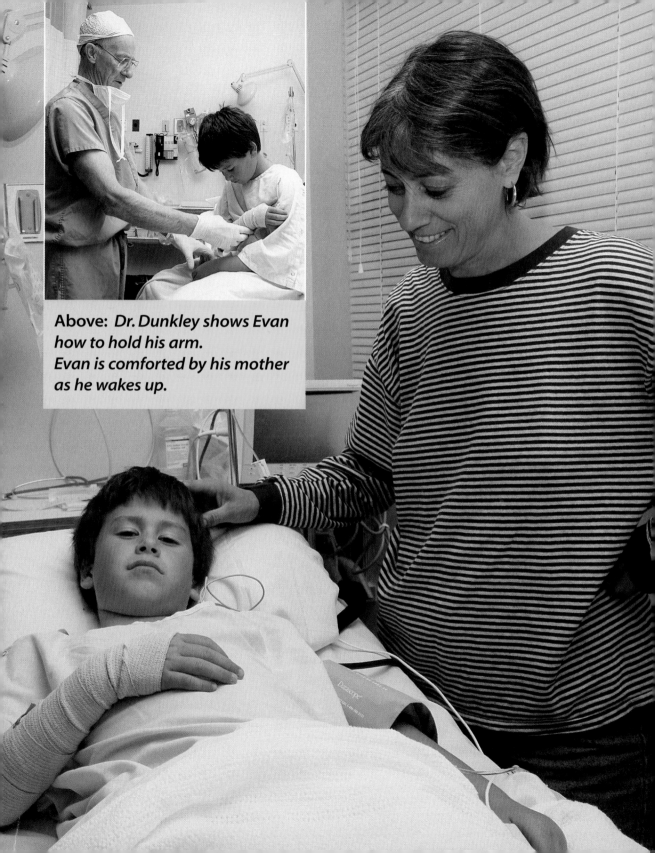

Above: *Dr. Dunkley shows Evan how to hold his arm.*
Evan is comforted by his mother as he wakes up.

By 6:00 P.M., Dr. Dunkley is back home. There is just enough daylight left for him to check up on his honeybees. This is one of his favorite ways to relax. With the pressures of his job, relaxation time is very important. Later in the summer he will collect several hundred pounds of honey. Over the years, his honey has won lots of prizes. In the winter, he makes candles from the beeswax.

Dr. Dunkley has just checked the last hive when his beeper goes off. There's been a moped accident. The ambulance is carrying a woman with a possible broken leg. Dr. Dunkley heads back to the hospital.

Relaxing with the honeybees.

By 8:30 at night, Dr. Dunkley is ready to head home. Just as he is leaving, he hears his name over the loudspeaker. He is wanted in obstetrics. This is the department where babies are delivered. A woman in labor has just arrived and needs relief.

"Oh thank goodness you're here, Dr. Dunkley," says Mrs. Chester. "The pains are every five minutes. Can you help?"

Mrs. Chester wants a regional pain block called an epidural. This will numb her from the waist down. In moments, Mrs. Chester is resting pain-free.

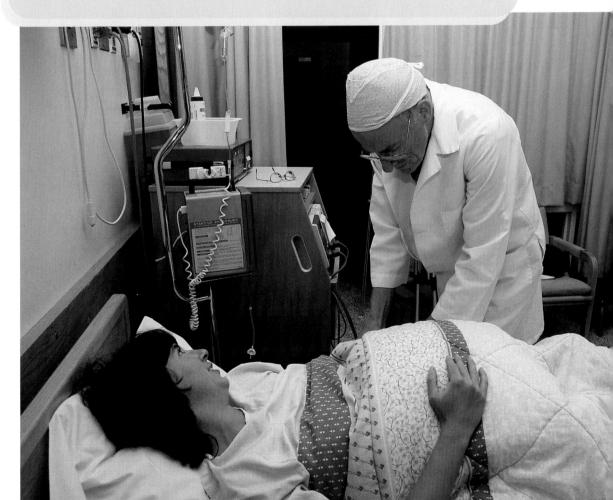

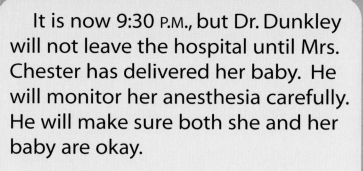

It is now 9:30 P.M., but Dr. Dunkley will not leave the hospital until Mrs. Chester has delivered her baby. He will monitor her anesthesia carefully. He will make sure both she and her baby are okay.

Dr. Dunkley tells a nurse that he will be napping, in case Mrs. Chester needs him.

Lying on a cot in the doctor's lounge, Dr. Dunkley thinks about his day. He recalls all the different people he's been able to help. At last, the doctor who puts the patients to sleep is able to grab a few minutes of sleep himself. It has been a long day.

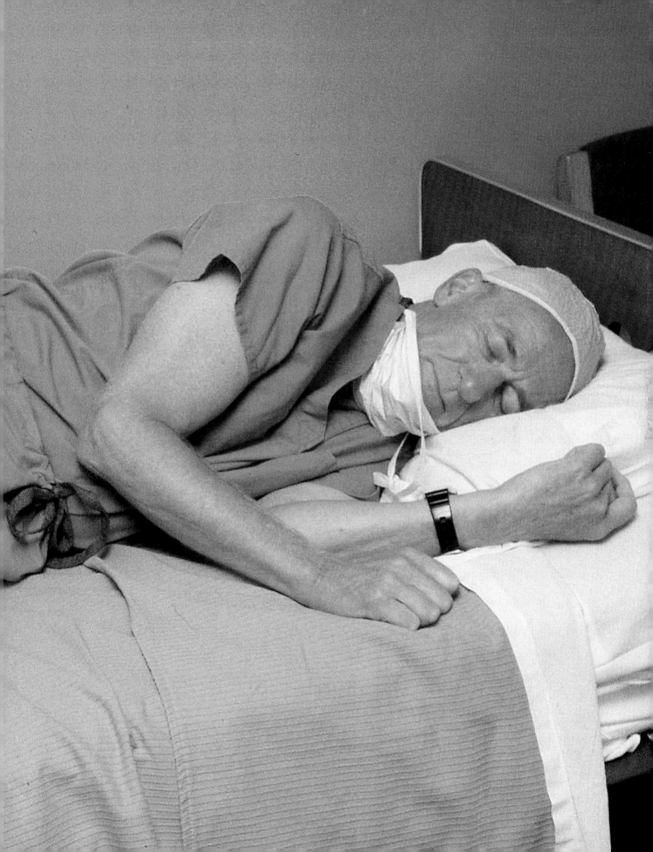

Glossary

anesthesia (an·es·te·jia) A special group of drugs that block pain in the body.

epidural A regional pain block that numbs a patient from the waist down.

intravenous (in·tra·veen·us) "Through the veins." An IV delivers medicine through the veins.

operation (op·er·a·shun) The cutting open of a body to fix or take out a damaged part.

patient (pay·shent) Someone being treated by a doctor.

sterile (ster·rill) Germ-free.

surgeon (sur·jun) A doctor who performs operations

unconscious (un·con·shus) Not awake; and unable to think, feel, or see.

Further Reading

Howe, James. *The Hospital Book.* New York: William Morrow & Company, 1994.

Lee, Barbara. *Working in Health Care and Wellness* (Exploring Careers series). Minneapolis, MN: Lerner Publications Company, 1996.

Miller, Marilyn. *Behind the Scenes at the Hospital.* Chatham, NJ: Raintree/Steck-Vaughn, 1996.

Ready, Dee. *Doctors* (Community Helpers series). Danbury, CT: Children's Press, 1997.

Index